AF472248

The Journey

The story of navigating a critical illness told through prose and poetry.

Helen Kerner

Published by Lulu
ISBN 978-1-4303-2019-7

Dedicated in gratitude to my

beloved husband, David W. Edward

and

loving son, Jonas M. Hinckley

This shaking keeps me steady. I should know.
What falls away is always. And is near.
I wake to sleep, and take my waking slow.
I learn by going where I have to go.

The Waking
Theodore Roethke

Table of Contents

INTRODUCTION

This collection of prose and poetry describes my journey from the stunning diagnosis of Leukemia in 1993, when I was told I had between three and five months to live, through the treatment of the disease and the renewal of my life and spirit.

For years I struggled with how to tell the story, how to share what I'd experienced in a way which might encourage others facing a similar predicament. I began by writing a detailed narrative which soon became too dense, too clinically focused, when what I wanted to share was more than simply a story of physical survival.

Nothing gets one's attention, wakes one up to life like the threat of impending death. Denial is an easy, sleepy place to be. But, suddenly like a tuning fork struck hard, every cell in my body came alive and to attention. From that exquisite pain came the courage to look squarely into the eyes of fate and be willing to participate fully in whatever might come, one breath at a time. Walking through the process was the most profound experience of *living* I can imagine.

My husband, David Edward, and I have developed a course, **After The Shock: The Journey - Navigating Critical Illness**, including twelve principles we followed during our experience. Several of my poems are featured in our presentation which has been presented at the Chautauqua Institution in upstate New York.

This book includes the entire collection of my poems about the journey.

ACKNOWLEDGEMENTS

Profound thanks are due to the many individuals who walked through this experience with us and who have encouraged me, supported me, and lovingly admonished me to gather this collection of poetry in book form. All lended heart as they were able, some furnished the rooms we lived in, some nourished our bodies, some comforted our spirits, and some read my poetry as it evolved. Each contributed to healing.

Though I cannot mention everyone by name, it is important that I acknowledge a few people without whom, not only would this collection not be here, my body would likely not be here.

First and foremost by husband, David Edward – the illness struck before we were married, yet he traveled with me every step of the way, enduring his own journey while staying accountable to his professional responsibilities. Together we developed a keener awareness of the value of conscious living and have since designed our lives accordingly. He was an inspiring partner in developing our formal presentation, and he is a great co-presenter.

The second most important person to thank is my younger brother, Manson Kerner, whom we still affectionately refer to as "*Marrow Man*". His gift of blood via a bone marrow transplant, restarted my crimson factory and saved me from a leukemia death.

Other muses to health and poetry include Elinor Bannwart, Nancy Barker, Dale Biron, Ida May Brown, Bo Burlingham, Lindy Edward, Emily Evans, Mollie Fisk, Peter Harris-Kunz, Terry Johnson, Martin Kerner, Karen LeVasseur, Joe Maio, Cora Nelson, Percy Randle, Kevin Wilson, Angela Winningham, Barbara Young, and too many other teachers, family members, and friends to mention by name ---- you know who you are.

Finally, to all the staff at Fred Hutchinson Cancer Research Center in Seattle, I give praise and thanks.

SYMPTOMS

An ancient principle reminds us to look for salvation in the darkest, most painful parts of our lives. We emerge into the light not by denying our pain, but by walking out through it.

Guilt Is The Teacher, Love Is The Lesson
Joan Borysenko

Our effort is our attitude toward life. If we have always met life as a struggle, thinking of ourselves as warriors in a battle instead of pilgrims on a path, healing will continue to make life an emergency.

Healing Into Life And Death
Stephen Levine

THE JOURNEY BEGINS...

Over Memorial Day weekend, 1993, we drove from Morristown, New Jersey, to Wake Forest, North Carolina, our new home. The company David worked for had relocated and we were looking forward to a Southern adventure. We spent the first few weeks in a motel, David going to the new office every day, me going to work at the new house, supervising minor remodeling and cosmetic changes prior to having our belongings delivered.

As the massive moving truck lumbered up the narrow driveway, waves of nausea hit me hard. I suspected exhaustion.

Symptoms ebbed and flowed during the entire summer, until finally we knew something beyond exhaustion or a minor virus was afoot.

As the symptoms appeared and disappeared while continuing with regular doctor appointments to monitor my blood counts, I conducted an investigation of my own, searching library medical reference books and devouring pages of new and used books at bookstores. I was thirsty for any clinical or physiological information about blood cells, blood production, and blood diseases. This was before the incredible resource of the Internet .

SOUTHERN SUMMER

My first Wake Forest June
splitting headaches, chattering teeth visit
nights more often than dreams. I wonder
at this climate's canned-air living.

In July every breath slices into lung.
At theater's intermission, dizzy, I scramble
over laps, push through the lobby crowd, slump
inelegant to the curb grateful for the night's cool air.

Nausea follows first taste of soup. I bolt
for the Ladies', hang my head over pocked porcelain,
wretch pink bisque into the bowl.

By August, knee and hip joints ache
as if tied to bone by wire. I consult a doctor:
"Nothing serious, a passing virus."

In September blood tests confirm
too few white soldiers defend against invader.

Myriad ailments tested and rejected:
Mono, Lupus, Epstein-Barr, Arthritis,
Bronchitis, Hepatitis, Lyme, AIDS.

October's restored vigor belies soldiers'
persistent dying in Indian Summer's heat.

FIRST MARROW EXAM

I peel off my clothes, try to remember
which is back, which front. Hands shake
locating armholes in the thin gown.

The room is cold. *"Lie down"*
The steel bed is cold. *"Curl into a fetal position"*

I imagine myself a pink shrimp on a bed of ice.

"Get comfortable"
'Yeah, right!' I want to flip sarcastic
hold my breath instead.

The first strike of pain an arrow in my spine.
I brace against the pressure, try to shut my ears
to the grind of needle mashing into bone.

Blood spills, pools warm at the small of my back.
Eyes seep tears, mind rattles gibberish of panic and fear.
Finally, only neon flashing lights: *my god, my god, my god!*

I gasp and wheeze. *(no meditative breathing here)*

The doctor mutters, unsatisfied.
I brace for more.
She tries again. And again.
Tolerance leaks out.

She will settle for a splinter of bone.
"Getting it will be less painful"
she promises.
But, she lies.

A chip of hip clinks into the cup.

"Can you handle one last aspiration attempt?"

She pats my haunch.

Now I am a mare on a stable floor.

I groan, grunt assent
and curse my obsessive courage.

Curled body unraveled
the nurse coaxes me back into position.

"You're doing so well"

Her cool palm brushes my hot forehead.
An abandoned child, I devour
the smallest notice of my effort.

Tears soak the pillow.
I taste salt, squint tight, hold my breath again.

FALSE ALARM ?

Between dire predictions
and swift dismissals of doom

I glimpse the love
I've always yearned for.

Weeks of ups and downs
ebbs and flows of speculation,

tides of irritations --- you
as distracted by potions and lotions

as I am by emotions.
One pool spills into another.

Monday on the verge of death
Wednesday nothing serious.

Another day forgetting
remembering in a rush of tears.

Between dire predictions
and swift dismissals of doom

I glimpse the love
I've always yearned for.

Am I Peter crying "Wolf!"?

DIAGNOSIS

Once more, Body, Old Paint,
how could you trick me like this
in spring's blowzy arms?

Relearning The Language Of April
Maxine Kumin

INVESTIGATION...

After we realized something more serious than a virus was going on, David accompanied me to every doctor appointment. We often compiled a list of detailed questions inspired by my various investigations, sometimes faxing them in advance so the doctor would be prepared for us.

From our General Practitioner we were referred to an Oncologist who gave an initial diagnosis of Lymphoma, followed by a withdrawal of that diagnosis and assurances that my condition was less severe, though still not definitive. She "*guessed*" a steroid treatment "*might*" resolve my symptoms. We declined her recommendation and asked for another opinion. A definitive diagnosis of Myelodysplasia transforming to Acute Myeloid Leukemia followed with a recommendation for *immediate* hospital admission and chemotherapy treatment. We declined because of information I'd discovered during my research. We asked for a third opinion including diagnostic confirmation and options for treatment. We were referred to a nationally recognized Leukemia expert in Baltimore, who confirmed my own research: even if I had aggressive chemotherapy it would likely not lead to permanent remission and my best option for "cure" would be a bone marrow transplant.

Coincidentally my two brothers, potential matches for transplant, both lived near Seattle where the Fred Hutchinson Cancer Research Center had on staff Dr. E. Donnall Thomas, the Nobel Prize winner who developed the bone marrow transplant process.

Such were the spiritual signs directing us.

DREAM AND DIAGNOSIS I

Inside a house with white walls,
white beams, and white carpet, radiant
light filling shadowless space
I am wrapped in white gauze,
dragged face down through a hallway
into a large, glass-walled room. Pulled
backward by my ankles by an unseen being,
arms outstretched, palms down, crimson stripes
on lush carpet mark my path. I slowly rotate,
turn face up, revealing tracks of deep wounds.
Blood bubbles, spills, soaks into pure white.

The doctor shapes her words carefully:

"I think it's Lymphoma."

Silence holds her message in the air.

Punched hard, stomach roiling
I want to bend forward, curl tight,
invisible. But do not move a muscle,
concentrate to hold the doctor's gaze.

She edges closer to my chair
leans in to explain her plan,
defining steps for confirmation.

Through fog we find the elevators.
Skin tight as dried mud, vise-hold
on composure, I stand stiff among the living.

FOLLOWING FIRST DIAGNOSIS

We stop for lunch. Tears
salt our salads while expressing
gratitude for our time so far.

We smile in sympathy for our young waiter

    creeping up to our table
    quietly offering coffee, serving
    extravagance of dessert.

We laugh through tears,
know he probably assumes
we're engaged in the standard traumas

    argument
    divorce
    or someone else's death.

PRAISE

You fly off on business. I drive
to the hospital for confirmation
Lymphoma runs rampant.

Brave today, and comfortable
in solitude, fascinated private eye
forensically investigating.

The padded table glides slowly into
the diagnostic tube. 15 minutes and $1500
later, I'm driving through vibrating autumn.

Mesmerized by late afternoon's orange glow
breathing crisp air, I admire flagrant leaves.
A pathologist may be confirming lymphoma

but I don't care. Grateful for this magnified
feast --- all senses awake --- determined to approach
death praising life with every breath.

BOOK LOVING BROTHER

You visit during my most intense investigation.
No accident, you and I alone together
for the first time in, maybe, forever.

We wander Chapel Hill, scour the used book store
thick with the dusty scent of dry parchment.
Books lean on bowed shelves, piled high

against yellowed walls. Handwritten signs
point to topics along clogged arteries of aisles.
You wander to 'True Adventure'.

I pore over 'Medical Reference'. Eyes snag
on white spine splashed with red: "Life's Blood"
sings from a voice within.

I inspect the Table of Contents, read the back
blurb, thumb through pages stuffed with clinical
detail of blood's chemistry.

Hands shaking, I pay --- some intuitive knowing
truth in these pages illuminates
what is yet unknown.

You visit during my most intense investigation.
No accident, you and I alone together
for the last time in, maybe, forever.

NEWS

Voice buoyant with excitement
she delivers the good news. Lymphoma's
not an option, something minor's causing
trouble, enough time for vacation
and to plan effective protocol.

I call you, elated to share the news.
We cry in relief, plan our trip to Florida
extravagance of the Keys.

Relief drains stress like a storm sucks
the beach clear before a tsunami.

PREGNANT DAY

I wake early. You next to me
radiating warmth.   I ease close,
curl against the arc of your back, seek
skin-to-skin along our shared length
careful not to disturb your sleep.

Today another appointment
a new doctor,   fetal hope of finding
the key to the mystery in my blood.
I lay still,   absorb comfort from your heat,
the sound of your predictable breath
wisping in and out.

Imagine what we might know by the time
we share this bed again.   Whatever,
if conclusive,   better than the aching
ignorance of all these weeks. I smile
against your naked back, inhale and hold
a last breath deep before sliding
one foot at a time   into pregnant day.

DREAM AND DIAGNOSIS II

I ride inside the taxi, leaning against you
the street outside awash in crying, bloody babies.
Naked carnage of some catastrophe we cannot
fathom. Each wail tapers to a whimper until among
the bodies lying thick, only one squirms, arms
outreaching, beseeching me to save her. You hold
me as I open the car door wide, lean out to scoop her
up. Door slammed tight, the driver guns the car
forward through the dead.

1.

Two long hours among bald patients
before blood's story is deciphered.
Two long hours before the unadorned
gray walls and chilled air of the exam room.

Another hour, the doctor sweeps in wafting
stale corridor-air. His white hair, thick
as a woman's wig, matches starched coat hanging
from thin, sharp-shouldered height. Black-rimmed
glasses mask ferret eyes set deep under bushy brows.

I perch on the exam table, legs swinging,
innocent as a child.

He sits opposite, eyes no higher than my knees,
recites technical jargon of blood values, percentages,
counts and chemistries, cloaked in pedantic voice,
as if I am a student he must lecture:

"Myelodysplasia"
"Acute Myeloid Leukemia"
"3 to 5 months to live"

"fatal" ricochets around the room.

The sharp intake of my breath doesn't slow him.
He continues, eyes drifting up to glance off
my forehead, brush David's arm.

Alien words fall from his mouth as casually
as a coroner recording autopsy findings:

> *"The blood manufacturing system is malfunctioning,
> making blood cells that cannot mature. It's
> like having the world overrun with toddlers –
> they're very cute, but they're not productive
> and won't grow up to help the body's world function."*

Startled by his cruel choice of words,
the grotesqueness of the image, I shiver
remembering my prophetic dream.

I stare at his moving lips, listen hard
to his authoritative drone, the public address
system announcing my immanent doom.

2.

He straightens papers, jots notes.
Finally meets my eyes, his face so unchanged
I imagine he's a robot whose tape has run out.

David's strangled voice:

> *"Where the fuck did this come from?"*

3.

Nerves ragged,
emotions threaten to spill
over composure's fragile dam.

I fumble to dress,
tear the arm of my blouse
concentrate to suppress blurt of tears.

We drive slowly home,
hands clutched tight across the abyss
ghostlike in the green light of the dashboard.

KNOWN UNKNOWN

Every day we live our lives
no inkling a predator might strike.
Vacant sense, ignorant well being.
Blind to what festers, growing
stronger, waiting patient.

On a day when least expected
out of a clear blue late autumn sky,
news. What was known
all along. Refined intuition
foretold in dreams.

TELLING

1.

On the long drive home
we struggle with how to tell them, how to face
the twisted coincidence her daughter died
of an identical diagnosis years ago, at the age I am now.

I try to imagine my mouth shaping such cruel words,
a bitter adieu on the last night of their visit. Adrift
on waves of despair, jolted by the car's sharp turn,
the crunch of gravel, I realize we're home.

In the dim light of the garage
we sit like stones after the engine dies.
Glancing sideways, your face contorted
in a queer smile, you squeeze my hand.

In the too-bright light their faces flushed
in expectation we huddle around the kitchen table.
My voice from a distant planet shares the news.

Tears pool and spill. She struggles to stand,
navigates the circle, pulls me up
and wraps me in her arms.

I lean into her, ache for myself
and for her re-opened wound. My father rests
his head in cupped hands, sways side to side,
a boat adrift without an anchor.

At midnight I lay in your arms
too exhausted for more tears
too shocked to think
impatient for sleep's safe harbor.

2.

They hobble toward the gate, juggle carry-ons
threatening to capsize their fragile frames.
Turning like a drunk, I stumble
to the garage, find the car. Keys chatter
against the door before locating the lock.
I collapse into the seat, waves of sobs rush free.

3.

The thought of calling New Jersey
stops my breath. Oh to deliver this news
in person to rock you as we cry. Hands shaking,
heart pounding, bile rising, I dial.

Relief and disappointment mixed, I get your machine.
My voice quivers, squeaks to leave a message.
I drop the phone annoyed, wait in dread and yearning
for your call.

Sitting motionless on the deck in the cool air
I jump at jangling interruption, count
three rings before lifting the receiver.

"Hi Mom. Hey, what's up?"

I begin to cry, try to speak.
Patient silence. Your soft whisper,

"Hey, Mom. What is it?"

Grace escapes. I blurt out the news in a single breath.

Your low moan.   Silence stretches
until like a balloon inflating the thin skin
bursts.

> *"We've been through some tough stuff before, Sweetie,*
> *but this is the biggest yet."*

Your struggled breaths, ragged voice across the wire.

> "Yeah, we *have been through a lot before, Mom.*
> *And we've gotten through it. We'll get through this, too."*

We talk a little longer, cry intermittently,
confirm Thanksgiving plans
and dread sad good bye.

A live grenade in your flimsy rubber raft
I push you far from shore.

4.

News to deliver like a Town Crier. I postpone
phone calls to my brothers, decide friends will hear
the news by mail --- time to fortify against onslaught
of concern.

> *"...The days are particularly difficult right now.*
> *I have been diagnosed with Acute Myeloid Leukemia.*
> *Even as I write I feel weaker --- that I must be writing fiction,*
> *not fact. Know, dear friends, that my heart is well, even if my*
> *body isn't..."*

How simple to type these calm words
Town Crier, fingers burned to ash.

GAME

Rejecting the common
metaphor of *"war"* we adopt
analogy of *"game"*. I name
myself Captain of our elite contingent,
employ wits and faith before each play
weigh investigation, consider
common practices --- recommended
by the experts who manage the league.
But they gamble for stakes
no higher than what fame demands
while I play for my life.
No trophy but First Place
will do. I am Captain,
Fate fair referee.

OLD FRIENDS
for Angie

We used to joke
about the "walking wounded",
the ones who cradled broken hearts,
crimson dripping
from their once-white sleeves.
We used to say
"die, so I can write about it",
joking-on-the-square
you called it.
Now here we stand,
at the other end of youth ---
knowing all about dying,
that one will go
before the other anyway,
so may as well write
while there's still time,
so we can laugh
loud together
in the face
of the nightmare
approaching.

MY BROTHER'S BONES

We were 3,000 miles apart when leukemia was confirmed.
With the diagnosis came an eerie calm, as if slapped into myopia
by a stone clapped hard against my head.

I called him from the car on the way to Chincoteague
where the wild horses roaming on sand-swept flats
breathe the clean salt air off the Atlantic.

Called him out of the clear blue sky, surprised to find
him at his desk on that ordinary Friday, to tell him
I was dying and his help was needed.

I repeated all the words the doctor'd said, as if I were a journalist
reviewing casualties of war, shards of truth embedded
under someone else's skin.

He listened hard, wasted not one breath when asking what to do.

Continuing down that long, wide road toward the Atlantic
I imagined a herd of thick-maned horses galloping out to greet me.
By Monday we would know if his bones held ore to mine.

God, grant me the serenity
to accept the things I cannot change;
the courage to change the things I can;
and the wisdom to know the difference.

The Serenity Prayer
Reinhold Neibuhr

TREATMENT

The more controlling we are, the harder it is to let go so as to see our shadow gradually, and the likelihood increases that we will heal by crisis. In crisis, we quickly learn that we cannot win alone. We need the help of friends and the grace of God. In our healing, we learn to ask for help.

Guilt is the Teacher, Love is the Lesson
Joan Borysenko

Because healing, like spiritual awakening, is such a creative matter, such a brailleing along individual pathways, one must sense wholly what is right for oneself.

Healing Into Life And Death
Stephen Levine

all those annulled connections
all those missed chances
and time running out untested.

Regret
Maxine Kumin

THE HEART OF THE JOURNEY...

On the Monday following Friday's firm diagnosis in Baltimore we learned my younger brother, Manson, was a near perfect match to be a marrow donor. Elated and terrified, our path was well lit and the hard work of the journey began.

The doctor who originally wanted me to be immediately admitted for chemotherapy became a helpful advocate for swift referral to the Fred Hutchinson Cancer Research Center in Seattle. We were given a December 3 appointment for evaluation and initiation, just 3 weeks hence.

During those short weeks, financial arrangements, medical directives, power of attorney, a will, David's work, all personal business including multiple phone calls to friends and relatives had to be arranged --- and Thanksgiving was to be celebrated when Jonas flew down to North Carolina from New Jersey.

The most surreal part of this time was sincerely preparing to die, accepting that I might never see my new North Carolina home again, my family, my friends. At this time, my health seemed so very good --- all symptoms of illness had miraculously abated.

Once in Seattle, we were enlisted in a strict regimen of appointments, examinations, explanations, meetings, tests, etc., along with the challenge of securing a temporary home within walking distance of the hospital where I would be required to live for at least 100 days post transplant. We arrived in Seattle on December 3; I was admitted to the hospital on December 20.

UNCHARTED TERRITORY

1.

When I sit down to write my will,
no idle future to delay me,
quiet strength infuses mindful distribution
meager cache of worldly goods.
Bank accounts and real estate be damned
important things demand more thought ---
which friend will bear the weight
of favorite earrings dangling from her lobes,
which savor the slide into sleek designer dress,
which protect and save the drawers of letters, folders
stuffed with poems until my son matures
          yearns to know his mother better.

2.

Like all explorers in uncharted territories
without a map or clue, no trail blazed
this way before, a road's bend may disguise
dead end, river's curve hide Niagara Falls.
Alone even when surrounded, engulfed
in palpable, pitying love. Behind
shadowed eyes, my impending death.
(Or so they seem to think)
Close friends
(or so I thought) look
straight through me, regard me
from a distance (when they dare)
as if I am already
          not there.

3.

I laugh amused at end-game power
my sad predicament
sweet lament
melancholy reality;
Fate has intervened
wrested my attention,
my intention now to prowl
this new territory, this sharp edge
closest to the end
          more alive than ever.

4.

When I sit down to write my will,
no idle future to delay me,
quiet strength infuses mindful distribution
meager cache of worldly goods.
Bank accounts and real estate be damned
important things demand more thought ---
which friend will protect and save the drawers of letters,
folders stuffed with poems until my son matures
          yearns to know his mother better.

HEAVY HAND

What trips us up on our way toward salvation? Paperwork. Absurdly, the need for guarantees, assurances, promises of payment trump all imperatives of impending death. *"It is sad you've got this awful disease, but tell us how you'll pay."* Sally, Captain of the Bureaucratic Finance Team, gloats in perceived superiority. Never mind faxed insurance company documents and bank guarantees assuring her of our funds. *"No, no!"*, she cries, *"only the originals will do."* Like some old witch in a nasty cartoon --- Cruella deVille in the flesh. What creepy power she enjoys. When home at night, I wonder if she rubs her hands in glee, having thwarted another dying person's attempt at timely treatment? The proverbial fly in the ointment, object of displaced rage and frustration, she, the necessary vent for my pent up stress. Steaming with pugilistic determination we ignore her weak defense, her blustering obfuscations, fly West without permission, to keep our first appointment while mourning those less belligerent than I who may die by this pencil-clutching bureaucrat's heavy hand.

RECEPTION

The elevator doors glide open
chunk to a stop,   inviting us to step
into the library-silence of the waiting room.

From behind the reception desk, a young woman
greets us in familial warmth, her smile open, unyielding,
unlike the glances of my friends   who dare not rest
their eyes on mine.

I scan the faces of other waiting pilgrims, some bald,
some scarfed,   some young,   some old; some gripping
metal poles on wheels dangling bags of dripping fluid,
some murmuring with companions, some slumped
hugging pillows,   some sitting alone in stiff silence.

Beyond mammoth plate-glass windows, Puget Sound.
The water calm, the sky dark   thick with swollen clouds,
as normal as any December day in a hundred years.
The large room even in the gloom   a cave of safety
before the storm begins.

ORIENTATION

We perch on hard chairs
children on the first day of school.
I stare at each face, guess who is patient,
who family or staff. Three settle into chairs
facing the room now quiet as a church.
The Director of Social Services smiles
like the Cheshire cat, invites introductions
if a patient, please share your diagnosis.

Dave from Moses Lake, burly, jaundiced,
defiant after a desperate year, found a donor
in Denmark. Acute Myeloid Leukemia.
His wife sits at his side, still as a stunned doe.

Bob, Apache from the reservation near
Phoenix, tall, slender, boyishly handsome.
Chronic Myelogenous Leukemia. His donor brother
with him, stocky contrast, a dancer and a fullback.

Tom, a stub of a balding, mustachioed man, a bartender
from a western movie. Multiple Myeloma. "I used to sell
the poison we'll be taking." He laughs, shakes his head,
drums a carved cane on the floor.

Last, my voice holds to say my name and diagnosis.
"And now, let me introduce my brother, Manson,
whom we affectionately refer to as Marrow Man".
Laughter erupts. Manson quips *"This isn't exactly*
the excuse I'd have wanted to spend more time with Helen."
Again, laughter. David, sheepish, *"I keep wondering*
if there's been a terrible mistake. Maybe she really isn't sick at all."

More laughter, gentle now, fading
until we all sit again in silence.

GOSPEL

When you
are introduced
as "Chaplain"
my curiosity dozes.

When you say
"I'm Percy
and I'm 10 years
post transplant"
my ears and heart
break open
at this good news:

Survivor come to share
hope of resurrection.

DIFFERENT GIFT

You come bearing
enough paraphernalia
to stay a month, though
we only planned the weekend.

The bathroom blooms
with your gear
like mushrooms
growing in the dark.

I accepted your
kind offer to help
make this place a home
before I am admitted

so after discharge (if I return)
the familiar will be a comfort
during the 100 days
I need to stay nearby.

Dear, well intended friend
I had forgotten
how vivid
our differences.

You sit silent on the rented sofa,
write quotes on cards to inspire
my recovery. I fold linens
and organize cleaned cupboards.

BLOOD DRAW

I stand near the glass door
waiting to be called, stare
at the patients sitting across
from white-coated technicians
wielding needles, labels, vials,
efficient as a military drill.
Invited to a chair, the technician
asks if I have a "*Hickman*". Having
never heard that word before, I shake
my head from side to side. She gently
beckons for my arm, cradles it under hers
firm against her side, taps for a vein,
reaches for the tools of her trade.

*"This is your first blood draw with us,
isn't it?"* Her liquid brown eyes lock
on mine, full lips forming warm smile.
I nod. *"Welcome,"* she whispers soft as a prayer.

MONICA

Eight month old
brown-eyed beauty
from Florida. Daughter
of a Cuban and Caucasian,
hard-to-match mixed-blood
extraction. Unprecedented
campaign for like-kind donors
won salvation's prize: a Faberge
egg in a field of grass at Easter.

Her ancient spirit electrifies
a room. One thousand watts
of wisdom must course through
her tiny veins. It cannot be Leukemia.

One moment a child's
whimper at procedure's pain
the next a Dalai Lama giggle.

She teaches us well
to live in the now, to feel
Grace in slivered seconds.

LIFELINE 1-3

1.

If you'd have told me I'd have a double-headed rubber line embedded in my chest leading directly to my heart, through which all manner of fluids will flow in and out: antibiotics, pain meds, chemotherapy, blood, nutrition, even my brother's marrow, well I'd have told you you were reading too much science fiction. I'd had an IV stuck into veins in arms to give hydration or take blood, but never anything more Frankensteinian than that. They call it a 'Hickman' (named after the doctor who invented it --- *and became rich*) and assure me it's the only way for the many infusions --- a direct line, no confusion --- to my heart as efficiently as possible. They confirm it will ensure an opening remain – to sustain the critical steps in my rescue process. I have the operation, follow directions to the T, except they didn't tell me to ignore the sore after and move my arm to keep it limber. So, my shoulder in a sling, freezes up. An angry redness comes --- my first use of this contraption? For antibiotics against the inflammation. So I have a permanent, dangling double-piped tube hanging from my chest. For which some doctor had invented (*and became rich*) a simple steel necklace clamp to keep it limp, and another doctor, designed the plastic cap (*and became rich*) to hold it firm against my skin to protect against infection. I take a class (which I have to pass) for cleaning the site and flushing, a ritual required *every day* to avoid infection rushing.

2.

Once installed and clear, the appendage I thought would freak me out forever becomes just another accoutrement of this weird adventure, a necessary evil, umbilical chord to healing. I lift it out as casually as another might pop open a locket to show a friend --- during the consultation with attending doctors, members of my family surrounding me, when they asked who the patient is, I flip out the line, twirl it like a pasty tassel, grin and say "guess who?"

3.

One time the Hickman bogs down in mid blood draw, clogs, refuses to allow the flow --- scares me stupid --- the only way to fix such a dilemma (I'd been told by a brave 5 year old who'd gone through it), is to "yank" it out, have a new one installed, like replacing an oil filter. After 15 minutes lying down the pressure changes inside me, I sigh in relief, avoiding any more grief when crimson squirts bright into glass tubes.

LAMINAR AIR FLOW LIFE

Behind a clear plastic curtain,
the bed, my island in this universe
suddenly perverse. Faces
come to visit or attend.
Fish on the other side of glass.

Gloves embedded in the drape
hang limp, dead wings of some
peculiar bird until a doctor
or a nurse inserts their hands
to animate the beast and touch me.

Sterile air flows quietly
pushing into, through
and out. Safe womb.
Umbilical I.V. nourishing
and healing me with poison.

Sole companion, Murray,
stuffed white bear dressed
in Christmas plaid
reliably good natured
in my arms at night.

I hold him tight, align
my breathing with the pump's
beep beep beep
Safe inside a special room ---
soft friend and a mother's heartbeat.

CHRISTMAS 1993

1.

My favorite season evokes such wrath today,
fierce resentment of the world *out there,*
where I no longer live. I live *here* now
behind this plastic curtain, in this sterile air.
I reject all good works of well-meaning volunteers
trying to buoy my spirits. They have no inkling
of what it's like in here.
Cheerfulness and Christmas carols,
gifts and colored lights --- disgust me.
My ire frightens them, I know,
but, I don't give a damn! If I die
I choose 1992 as my last Christmas ---
when excitement for the coming year came as easy as a sigh.
I could die peacefully, that being my last Christmas.
Take away that tiny tree!
Be gone all ye of good will!

Anger holds my sanity by a thread.

Next year, *if it comes,* I'll decorate *two* trees
but this year I'll have none.

2.

Red beam of radiation drills me deep
while you stand safe behind lead doors, chat and joke
as if waiting in a bakery for a Christmas cake.

3.

Christmas comes late this year ---
gift of marrow wrapped in plastic pouches,
hangs like stockings on the pump. Crimson creeps
down and up transparent tubes, through the Hickman
to my heart.

Gift of Life?
We'll know by Valentine's, next holiday of red.

HARVEST

4 chemo days
3 of full body radiation
'0' says it's harvest time
and your bones bear the crop.

Strapped to a steel gurney
wheeled into the sterile room
they drill deep into your hard
hips and back, suck out a little
of your life in hopes of saving mine.

Sore bones for several days,
your lost crop's restored long
before cells might sprout
in my fallow stroma.

HAIR TODAY GONE TOMORROW

1.

When I first peered at my image in a mirror ---
wispy halo ringing toddler head,
thin bangs protecting shy eyes
against the gaze of others ---
I could not see who was there,
          that there was a *me* to see.

My aunt once took the shears
and pruned me like a shrub.
Bangs nearly gone,
I stared into the glass all eyes --- stunned
          my *self* exposed.

2.

Before I take the poison I cut my hair
so patches of scalp won't gape
through random strands,
trees left standing in a fire's wake.

With my half inch of bristle
you might --- for a while ---
mistake me for a rock star
or a radical.

When needles of thatch
carpet my pillow,
head naked in reflection,
I'm relieved the cure is working
          and wonder *who* will be saved.

MY DEATH IN YOUR EYES

Concern's expressed, but your gaze belies
fear beneath, naked as a feral cat's.
I see my death reflected in your eyes.

Your visit will be short as I surmise,
the time fills up with silly, idle chats.
Concern's expressed, but your gaze belies.

Lacking truth, real talk dares not arise;
no prognosis, protocol, or stats.
I see my death reflected in your eyes.

Say you'll come again, I detect soft lies
my baldness repels under fancy hats.
Concern's expressed, but your gaze belies.

Sympathy rings false with all your tries.
There's no comfort in your timid pats,
I see my death reflected in your eyes,

loathe what determined cheerfulness hides,
reminds me of those old days and our spats.
Concern's expressed, but your gaze belies;
you see *your* death reflected in *my* eyes.

BREATHING IN THIN AIR

No better gift in life might I secure
inhaling deep into all moments, pure.
        How sweet each awakened breath
                before eternal silence of my death.

Roethke said it best,
grand prize of life's unrest: wake to sleep
        and take my waking slow, learn
                by going where I have to go.

Welcome Reaper, if it be my time,
I remain intrepid on this Everest climb
        I'll take each day and step in easy stride
                adoring Mystery like a faithful bride.

RECOVERY

Mindful of the hindrances to healing -- the doubt and fear and resistance -- we come to see how difficult it may be to let go of our suffering. We are so attached to it, we are so identified with pain in our mind/body as being who we are.

...

Our healing is as deep as our investigation.

Healing Into Life And Death
Stephen Levine

A NEW INTENSITY...

After the euphoria of discharge came a new reality, a daily focus and subliminal worry about germs, infection, medications, and relapse. The regime of self care intensified. Many patients required readmission to the hospital for one reason or another and we were determined not to enjoy that experience. My energy was very low and I could cognitively not yet manage all the self care activities, so David's responsibilities increased. Immediately after discharge I was still on daily hydration and I.V. nourishment. David's work load, both professionally and personally expanded. I required 24 hour care which meant that when he had to travel, I needed a "minder". I was on some 17 different medications that had different daily schedules, which included extremely high dose Prednisone which has a negative effect on personality, and the dressing on my Hickman site required daily freshening. Alternate days (and sometimes daily) I needed to shuffle the few blocks to the outpatient center for blood draws and other tests. This was to last, assuming no complications arose, for 100 days post transplant.

My strength improved over time and eventually I did manage to stay alone, even venture out into the world on my own, but it was a long, emotionally draining haul.

FREE AT LAST, JANUARY 18, 1994

1.

Discharged into the winter air,
neon dusk, lights so bright it could be Christmas.
Martin Luther King Day --- perfect day to celebrate my freedom.

You drive where I choose -- beloved Arboretum.
On winding roads we repeat the pre-admission trail
lush growth of green to the edge of Lake Washington. Glistening

mirrored shards reflecting sun's last light and I am alive
to breath the air across the lake and Puget Sound, salt and mist
mingling close as life and death. You drive. I stare and cry
in disbelief at such good fortune.

2.

I have yet to see a mirror. Wrapped a scarf
around my head before leaving the hospital, fancy
myself Louise Nevelson venturing into a new world.

Alone behind locked bathroom door, I stare unblinking
at the friendly alien, eyes awash in yellow, skin tanned
as if at the beach for weeks. No hair anywhere. No eyebrows,
lashes, or pubes. Curious stare from self somewhere. In there.

3.

After 28 dry days, the shower anoints
warm absolution. I stand still let water accumulate
in the tub, slide down for full immersion. Reborn water being now.
I vow to endure whatever mutation may be required
to live on familiar land again.

SHOWING UP

One foot
in front
of the other
shuffling
like a sleepwalker.
Half an hour
to outpatient
three blocks away.
The daily
draw of red
to tell
what condition
my condition is in.
One foot
in front
of the other
shuffling
like a sleepwalker.
I am no
somnambulant,
only a
determined
soul working
her way
slowly back
one step
at a time.

DIFFERENT DAUGHTER

For some time I'd yearned to see you.
When you finally come to visit
and I open the door, you look up,
squint and say:

"Jesus Christ, why don't you wear a wig?"

I guess you are shocked at my bald head,
yellow skin and albumin eyes.

I laugh as I have learned to at your habit
of speaking whatever truth flies
across your brain.

"I'm glad to see you, too, Daddy."

Who can blame you, seeing a different
daughter disguised so convincingly
in a shroud of grave infirmity?

LIFE AT THE CHARBONNEAU

We almost didn't find it
this temple of temporary living.
Almost walked on by, assuming
it too rich for our short term purpose.

We nest quick as squirrels
hunkering down for a long hard winter.

Weird being beeping in the night.
Phantom ankle pain, burning urination,
stranger in the mirror. And you, wanting
to make love to the monster that is me.

Every day vigilance, hand washing,
blood counts and prayers.

Other animals live like this ---
constant spikes of terror
at the breaking of a twig
or an abrupt flight of birds.

LIFELINE 4

4.

On a celebratory day in March, after being deemed beyond the need, the Hickman is scheduled for "*removal*". Well, as it turns out, a better term is the five year old's, "*yank*". Like a recalcitrant, deep-rooted weed, after joking about putting his foot on my chest, the nurse grasps the double white tube with both hands, as close as he can to where it exits my chest, advises me to hold onto the sides of the exam table, then pulls with mighty strength without anesthetic, or false promise of no pain. I grip the table as instructed and feel every fraction of tube tearing from the tissue encasement acquired during its 4 month stay inside. The pain, a wire burning through me. I barely hear his apology for why numbing and surgery would not suffice --- too long a slice from chest to heart --- the only way this forceful wrenching part. When done, I gasp and wince and catch my breath. Then wonder, what if a relapse should occur? But, such thoughts are swift and fleeting, I concentrate on fleeing!

TRAINING

White blood cell counts
focus our long Seattle days.
Through chemo and radiation

like dedicated fans
of some weird sport,
we root for a zero half-time score,

cheer for the downward slope,
groan at any upward surge.
Zero count achieved

my brother's blood, still warm,
pumps into me like farm team rookies
joining the big league.

We wait patient
for them to make their move.
As counts begin to climb

we begin to breathe again.
At 500, I win release from sterile room
to neighborhood. The goal now moved

from white cell counts to days outside.
At 100, promotion to the team back home.
Final goal to survive and improve.

My daily training?   Living.

HOMECOMING

We imagine that we must force results, must plow a path to freedom rather than discovering the ground beneath our feet. But by taking a step at a time and trusting the moment, we find that a step fully taken leads effortlessly to the next. By fully participating in this moment, the next moment takes care of itself.

Healing Into Life And Death
Stephen Levine

AS IF FROM THE MOON...

Leaving Seattle was incredibly difficult. It was my home town, where I had close friends and all my family. Fred Hutchinson had become my second and most sacred home. I feared being all the way across the country should I relapse.

Having barely settled in North Carolina, returning there felt foreign and strange. In addition, I knew few people and expected David would return to his prior work intensity. Because I had gained weight, swollen up, mostly bald but suffered severe hirsuteness and moon-faced as a result of the anti-rejection drugs, I felt self conscious and embarrassed, reluctant to go out in public. I did not bear any resemblance to the woman who had left four months earlier.

I had to reach deep into myself to find the courage to put one foot in front of the other, to trust the process and follow through. Returning to North Carolina having survived, oddly, was much more difficult than leaving to face treatment.

GOING HOME, APRIL 1

1. Seattle:

Alarm shatters 4 a.m. silence.
April Fool's Day but, no joke,
we're going home. Savoring
coffee's aroma, I pad bare-footed
into brightness. His back to the door,
my father sits stirring coffee, headphones
hugging ears, legs crossed, one foot
tapping to music only he can hear.
I slide my hand back and forth across
his bony shoulders. He looks up, grins,
tosses headphones to the table.

"Well. It's about time ya got up.
You've got a plane to catch."

Juggling steaming cups
we drag luggage to the car, pack
the trunk tight as bagged groceries.
Our breath, silver clouds in the crisp air.
At the airport we hold matching
blue-eyed gazes, share a lingering hug.

"I'm going to miss you, Daddy."

I begin to cry. He chokes.

"Okay, honey. You take care now,
ya hear? Just do what yer s'posed to
ta keep getting well"

He pats my back as if burping a baby.
Another quick squeeze
before I pull away.

"I love ya, honey"   *"Me, too".*

He staggers to his car, small and vulnerable
as a child about to be lost in a crowd.

2. Chicago:

Nauseous, dizzy
I escape the plane, lurch
into the lavatory
vomit.

3. Raleigh:

Wobbling on rubber legs
I navigate airport's confusion.
"Welcome Home" blazes
across the balloon-filled van.

"Lot's ah folks send they love, but ah cum alone.
Thought it'd be more comfterble for y'all."

Our friend beams. I flinch
at his accent, brace against
this Southern land. Rumbling
over the highway I lean into your shoulder,
try to remember our house, this friend,
the small town we call home.

4. Wake Forest:

"Sweetheart, we're here."

The white house sprawls across the hump
of land beyond the pond. Yellow ribbons encircle
several pines, bows hang centered on garage doors.
Trembling, I step into the kitchen.
Gaze sweeps vague familiarity. We walk gingerly
as cats through each room. Pots of flowers,
balloons, baskets of food tucked in unexpected places.
Crumpling to a chair, your warm hands
massage my neck as I sob.

SURVIVOR

An astronaut returned
determined to live normal

after visiting terrain few
have explored. Swollen face,

hairless head, yellow albumin
eyes. Squab fallen from the nest.

No lead boots holding fast
to old landscape's ashes.

Brailling new ground. Ground
foreign as the moon.

SQUALL

The day weighs heavy
a storm brewing inside.

The phone a stone.
Buttons resist finger's force
dialing your ten numbers. Miles
between us stretch near to breaking.

You lift the receiver
say your name.

My hoarse voice
"*Hi, Percy*" before I begin to cry.
"*Ah*", you say, "*Having*
one of those days, are you?"

You assure me
I will not drown.

Familiar with rogue squalls
your listening benediction
better than by any medicine
swallowed religiously each day.

CODDLER

She offered
new friendship
syrupy and sweet.
Emoted
understanding
for a person
maybe dying.

As if she could assuage
her own fear by helping
me with mine

I talked about her
arrogant attention, said
I was not a cripple
needing crutches,
a mental case
without opinion,
nor on my death bed yet.

She smiled
tolerantly
saw only bald
and swollen
other
requiring
her protection.

As if she could assuage
her own fear by helping
me with mine

A SON'S FIRST VISIT

Your first visit
since my return.
Jittery as a caffeine junky
anxious to see your face
I go alone to the airport to fetch you.

Did not think to warn you
the meds have had their way.
A squab fallen from the nest: wispy hair,
moon face, and bulbous yellow eyes
belie the recovery the doctor assures.

At the gate, your thin voice, "*Is that you, mom*?"

The photo from the day:
side by side sitting on the deck
you stare out eyes wide in horror
and confusion,   my distorted smile.
When diagnosed I appeared in robust health
and now this ugly bird.

CHECK UPS

Wary survivor, I travel monthly
to the doc who diagnosed me

hold tight fisted gut, brace
against bad news.

Drive home breathing deep
a swimmer saved from drowning.

At three month intervals
anxiety suppressed --- a mouse waits

in the dark, darts into the light
to hear good numbers read.

At six month cycles confidence
lifts its head, whistles in the dark.

Annually now, swimming far from fear's edge,
I trust the monster in the deep is dead
and not just sleeping.

RENEWAL

When you realize where you come from,
you naturally become tolerant,
disinterested, amused,
kindhearted as a grandmother,
dignified as a king.
Immersed in the wonder of the Tao,
you can deal with whatever life brings you,
and when death comes, you are ready.

Tao Te Ching
translated by Stephen Mitchell

THE END IS THE BEGINNING…

David and I are grateful for the illness that brought us to a clearer acceptance of life as it is presented to us and a consciousness with which we want to live it.

After our return to Wake Forest, we focused on my recovery and also on what the experience had taught us. We determined that life, being as unexpectedly interruptible as it is and as short as it is, demanded that we set a new course. We began to design a plan for our future that included getting David off the high-pressure career path and both of us living a more intentional, mindful life.

For my part, after the initial two years of recovery which brought me to within 98% of my former health and energy, I knew I no longer wanted to "work" in the traditional sense. I wanted to live more fully in each moment and to share my experience with others. Since that time I have counseled many people who have faced and gone through a critical illness like mine, several of whom have had bone marrow transplants. Not all have survived, but I believe my connection with each one was meaningful to them, and certainly to me.

David retired in 1999 and we moved to Marin County, California. Together we developed our presentation **After The Shock: The Journey - Navigating Critical Illness** which includes 12 defined principles and many specific tools we recognized in retrospect had aided our journey.

We enjoy winters in Mexico and fully live our lives one day at a time, grateful every day for the experiences that woke us up to the beginning in the end.

AMAZING GRACE

In the dark wet days
when I was still running,
drowning and running,
running to, then away,
joys denied accumulated
like balsawood on a funeral pyre.

I stood naked,
shredded rags at my ankles
despair crawling within
like lice under my skin.
Until Your light came.

Warm breath of You
gave me hope. Now
willing to walk
ascetic on the earth

wherever I go flowers
bloom along my path.
The closer I get to You,
the louder I hear
a hymn from a far-off choir.

Amazing Grace,
I am saved.

ABBE

We spoke often
in the months before your treatment.
I shared the details of my journey
as you prepared for yours, following
a protocol different from mine
in a place I would not have chosen.

We talked of God
and Grace and happenstance,
Fate's intention for us all. We
laughed and cried, let the line hum
empty for minutes at a time ---
so many miles between us.

I heard his voice
on the machine and knew.
Searched the Internet for confirmation
before calling him back. Found you
in the archives, your dark eyes
staring straight into mine, unblinking.

100 DAYS

Inspired by 'Ghosts of Rwanda'
PBS Frontline documentary, 2004

I sit mesmerized --- balloon of ignorance pierced
remembering my reality April 1, 1994.
My one hundred days
just ended when theirs began.

As machetes sliced black skin
their blood rushing through the tall
green grass of Africa, spilling hot
across the cold church floor

my brother's blood raced
through my veins restoring
me to privileged life.

While Hutus delivered death by intention
to their Tutsi brothers and sisters,
(the whites --- *even the dogs of whites* ---
airlifted from the menace)
I flew home to shape a mindful life.

One hundred days,
eight hundred thousand deaths.
The world argued over genocide's definition
while the madmen raged. The brave
who stayed walk the ground remembering
the smell and sounds of carnage.

I sit mesmerized --- balloon of ignorance pierced
remembering my reality April 1, 1994.
My one hundred days
just ended when theirs began.

I sit mesmerized --- balloon of ignorance pierced
breathing bitter air of gratitude and grief.

FOLLOWING
for Angie

Your voice on the phone sounds
as always,   melodic as a songbird
on the verge of laughter
                    but your message strikes me dumb.

Coarse fringe of dark humor, like dried blood
on a surface wound. Yet this is no surface wound
no casual split in skin;   a heart-deep bleed
                    promising steady, stubborn pain.

You think of me often, you say, remember
my journey years ago when you watched
as from far atop a hill,   until I disappeared
                    on my solitary odyssey.

Now, my turn to keep
vigil as you walk
into the shadowed unknown,
                    nothing but Grace to guide you.

RADIATION REDUX

For Victoria

I lounge under the Mexican sun
remembering. Appreciating
how far I've come from where
you are today.

I smell the hospital air, feel
the temperature drop, the elevator
thudding to the basement. See
the lead-lined room buried in the bowels
of the building waiting empty.

I walk beside you, shadow you,
breathe every breath
with you today.

LUXURIANT COMPLAINT
February 22, 2005 for Victoria

Agitated
life pounds
in my veins.
Recovered over
ten years. Now living
in too many places, distant
from beloved faces --- emails
race from coast to coast and across
the sea. How can it be? Living
such a life of luxury and me complaining.

Today
you lay
in a steel bed
praying for similar
rebirth. Hope the warp
and weft for those who may
be left bereft. Illness set our fate,
might yet prove your end. I pray every
day for luxury of life and you complaining.

RESOURCES

For more information about this book or the presentation **After The Shock: The Journey - Navigating Critical Illness**, please email hlkerner@gmail.com.

Order additional copies of this book on line at **lulu.com/HLKerner**. The book is also available from lulu.com as a download.

NOTE: This is a not-for-profit publication. All proceeds in excess of costs are donated to the Fred Hutchinson Cancer Research Center in Seattle, Washington.

www.ingramcontent.com/pod-product-compliance
Ingram Content Group UK Ltd.
Pitfield, Milton Keynes, MK11 3LW, UK
UKHW040601210726
13854UKWH00008B/1707

9 781430 320197